Italian for Beginners Kids

...A Beginners Italian Workbook, Italian for Kids First Words (Italian for Reading Knowledge) Volume 1

By

Amyas Andrea

COPYRIGHT NOTICE

Copyright © 2018 by **Amyas Andrea**.

All rights reserved. This book or any portion thereof may not be reproduced or used in any manner whatsoever without the express written permission of the publisher except for the use of brief quotations in a book review.

Cover by Eljays Design Concept

Printed in the United States of America

First printing July 2018

Table Of Content

INTRODUCTION 6

Meet Noel/ Incontra Noel 8

Numbers/ Numeri 10

More numbers/ Più numeri 20

Shapes/ Forme 23

Fruits and vegetables / Frutta e verdura 29

Body parts/ Parti del corpo 35

Days of the week/ Giorni della settimana 44

Noel : *Let's look at days of the week* 44

Days we go to school/ Giorni andiamo a scuola 45

The months of the year/ I mesi dell'anno 48

Twelve months of the year/ Dodici mesi dell'anno 49

Seasons of the year/ Stagioni dell'anno 50

Colors/ Colori 52

Animals/ Animali 53

Other common words/ *Altre parole comuni* 54

INTRODUCTION

Welcome to this simple English to Italian for beginners book.

You will agree with me that it is always better to go from the known to the unknown.

Therefore, in this book, you will learn about numbers, colors, shapes, days of the week, parts of the body and more in Italian language.

Learning Italian language has never been so easy...just try this simple book out.

Thanks for your interest in this small book. Now go ahead, get a copy for your kid! Enjoy.

Meet Noel/ Incontra Noel

Hello, my name is Noel/ *Ciao, mi chiamo Noel*
I am a boy/ *sono un ragazzo*
I am six years old/ *ho sei anni*

I love Italian language/ *Amo la lingua italiana*

And I think it is a great idea for you to learn how to speak Italian too!/ *E penso che sia una buona idea imparare anche a parlare italiano !*

So let's have some fun learning together! / *Quindi impariamo divertendoci insieme!*

Numbers/Numeri

Noel : *Let's start with **numbers***

Iniziamo con i numeri

Trace the number below/ Traccia il numero qui sotto

One   Uno

Trace the number below/ Traccia il numero qui sotto

Two   *Due*

Trace the number below/ Traccia il numero qui sotto

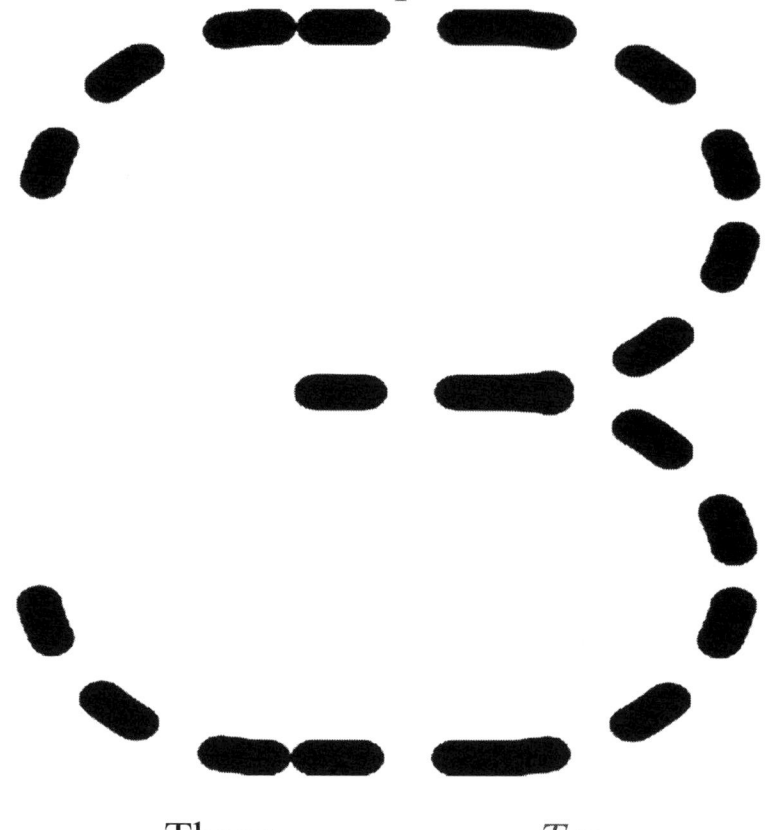

Three   Tre

Trace the number below/ Traccia il numero qui sotto

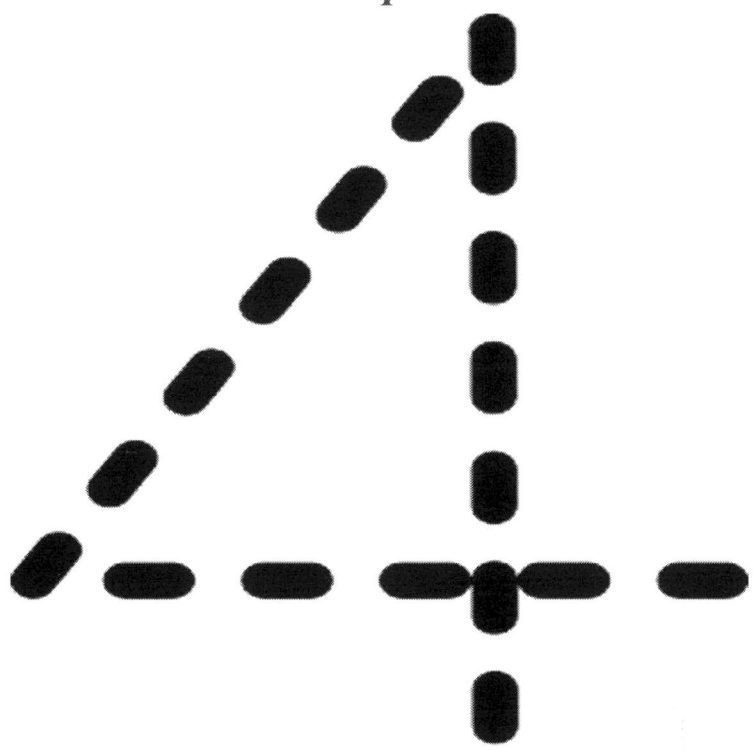

Four   *quattro*

Trace the number below/ Traccia il numero qui sotto

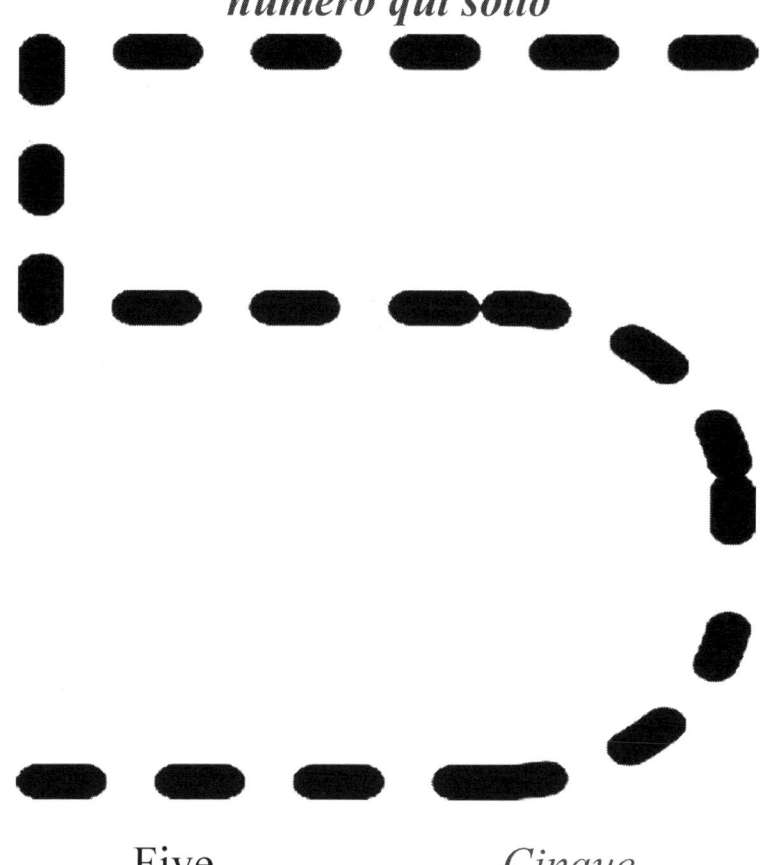

Five   *Cinque*

Trace the number below/ Traccia il numero qui sotto

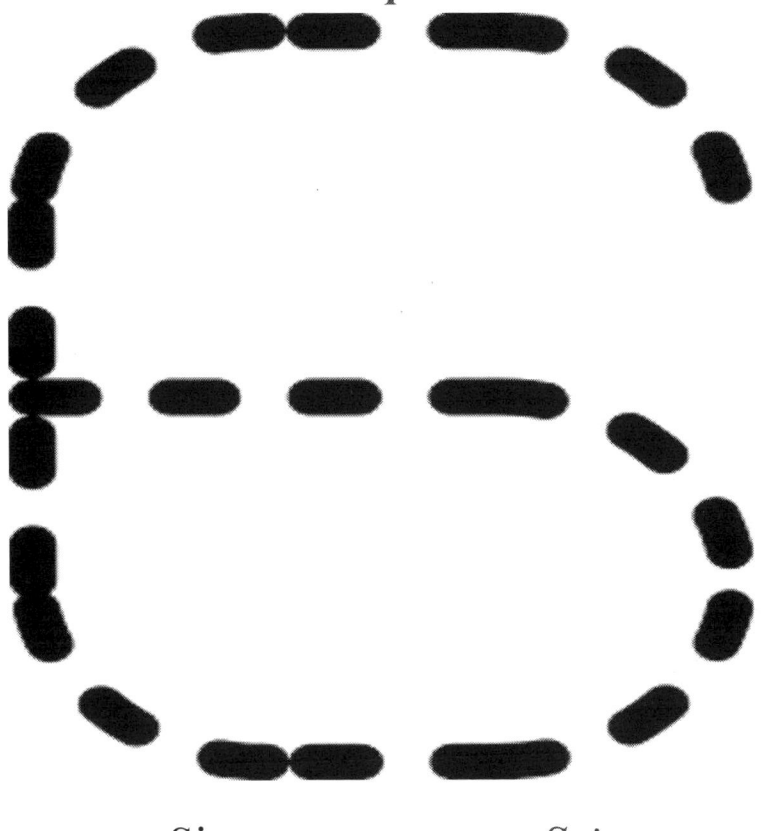

Six   Sei

Trace the number below/ Traccia il numero qui sotto

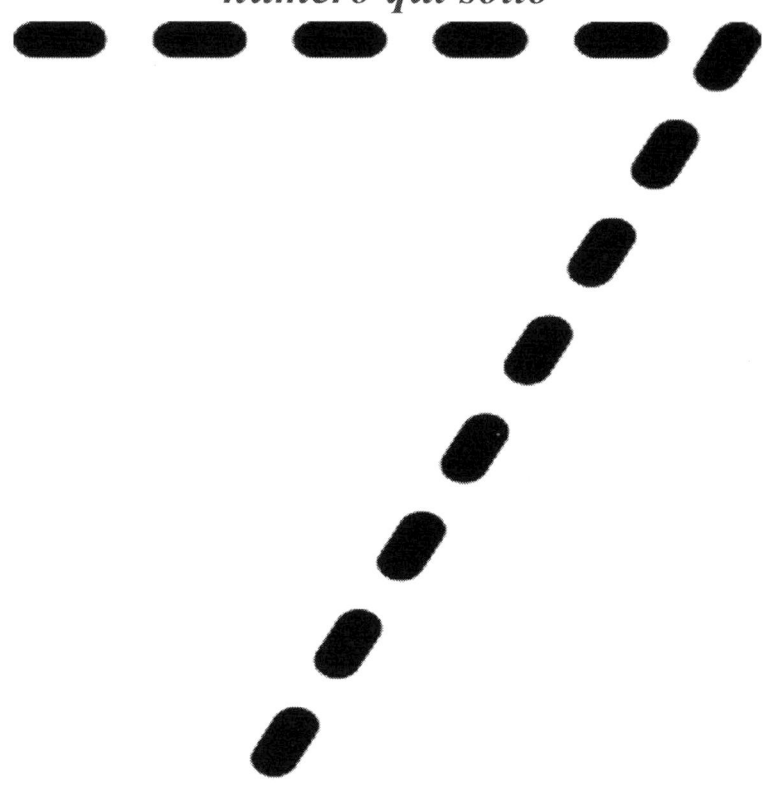

Seven -   Sette

Trace the number below/ Traccia il numero qui sotto

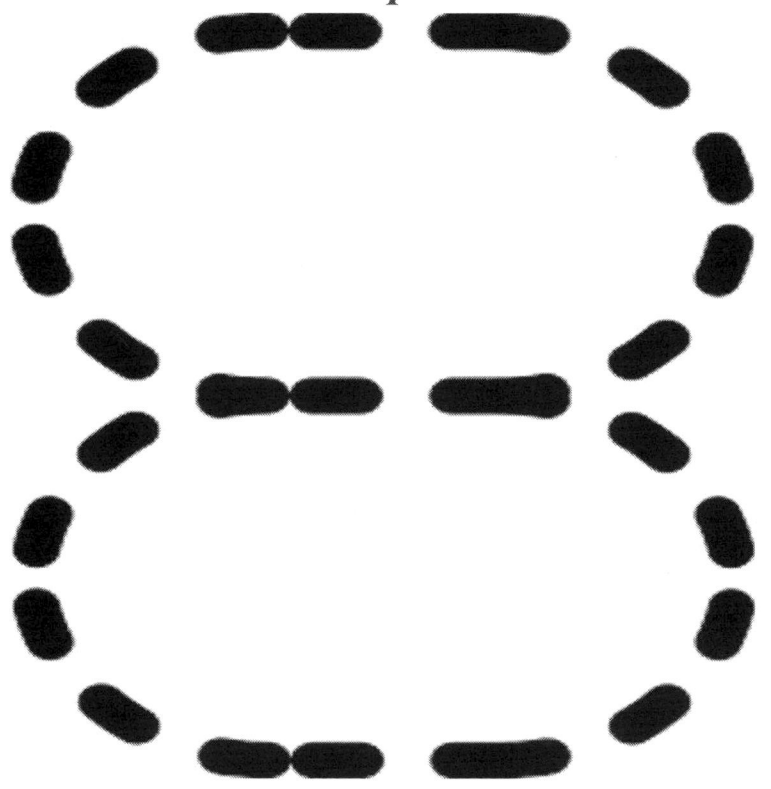

Eight -   *Otto*

Trace the number below/ Traccia il numero qui sotto

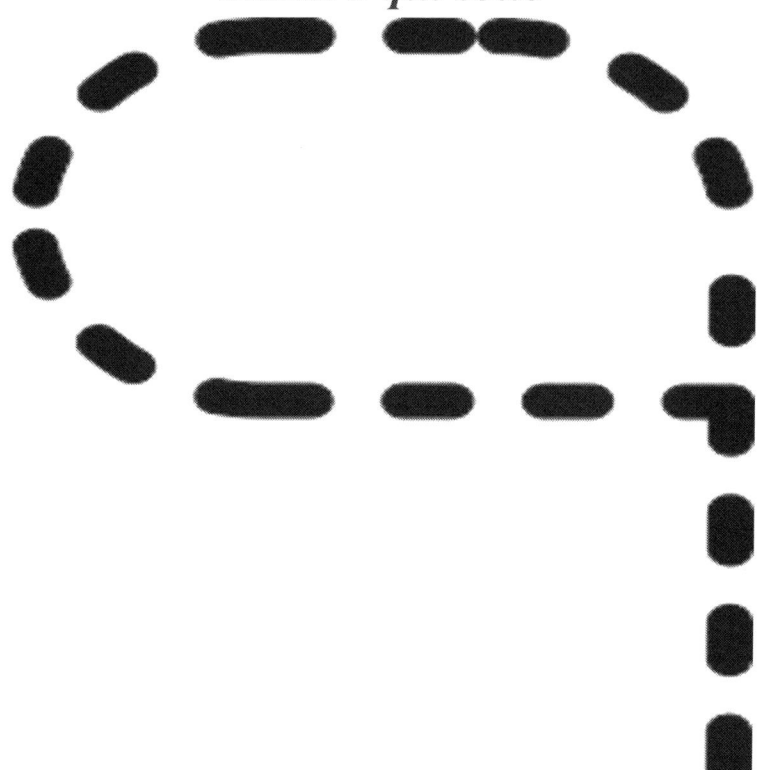

Nine -   Nove

More numbers/ Più numeri

Noel: More numbers

    Più numeri

Ten	*Dieci*
Eleven	*Undici*
Twelve	*Dodici*
Thirteen	*Tredici*
Fourteen	*Quattordici*
Fifteen	*Quindici*
Sixteen	*Sedici*
Seventeen	*Diciassette*
Eighteen	*Diciotto*
Nineteen	*Diciannove*

Twenty	*Venti*
Twenty-one	*Ventuno*
Twenty-two	*Ventidue*
Twenty-three	*Ventitré*
Twenty-four	*Venti quattro*
Twenty-five	*Venticinque*
Twenty-six	*Ventisei*
Twenty-seven	*Ventisette*
Twenty-eight	*Ventotto*
Twenty-nine	*Ventinove*
Thirty	*Trenta*
Forty	*Quaranta*
Fifty	*Cinquanta*
Sixty	*Sessanta*
Seventy	*Settanta*

Eighty	*Ottanta*
Ninety	*Novanta*
Hundred	*Centinaio*

Shapes/ Forme

Noel: Let's talk about shapes

Parliamo di forme

Square -   *Piazza*

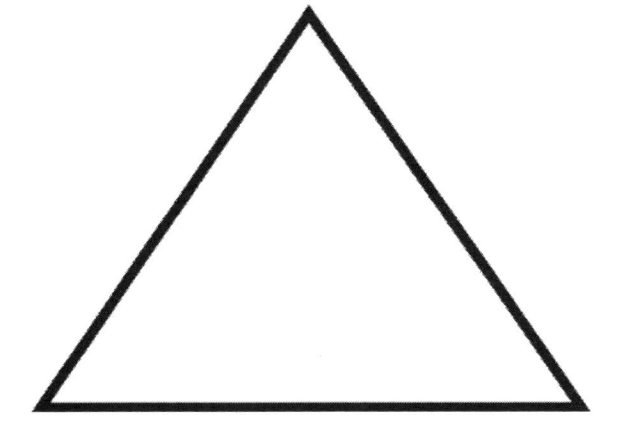

Triangle -   *Triangolo*

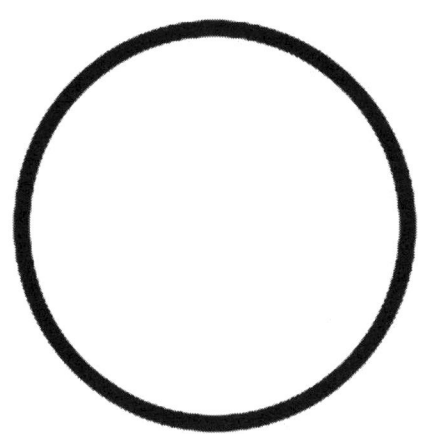

Circle -   *Cerchio*

Rectangle -   *Rettangolo*

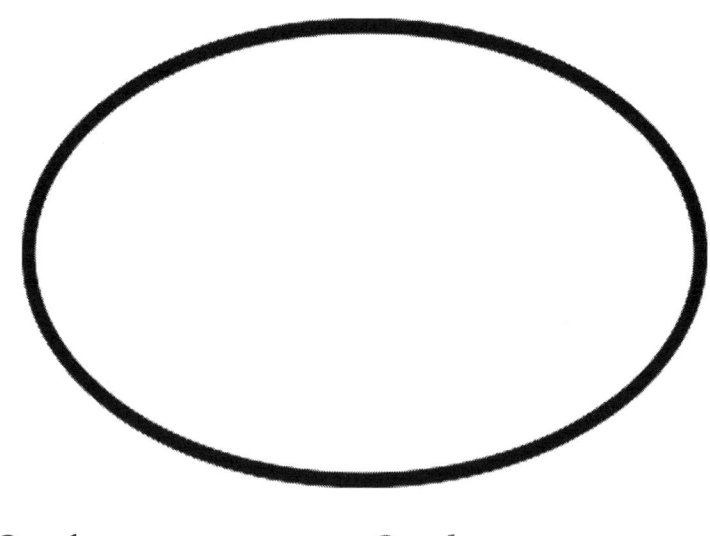

Oval -   *Ovale*

Trapezium -   *Trapezio*

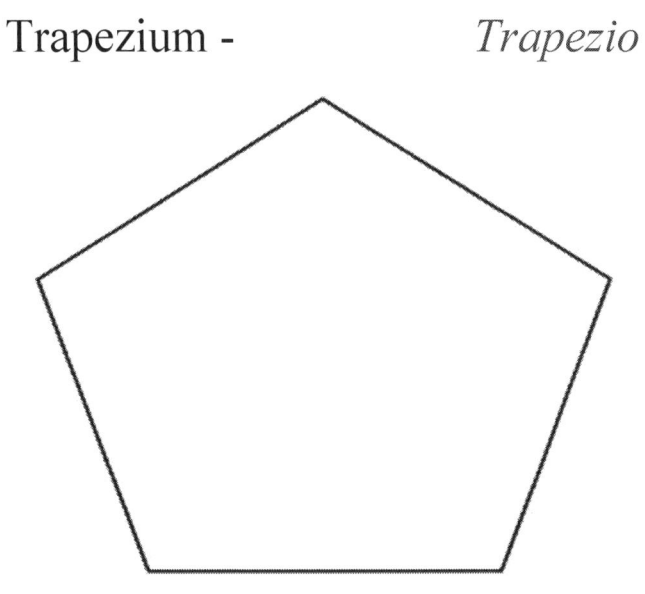

Pentagon -   *Pentagono*

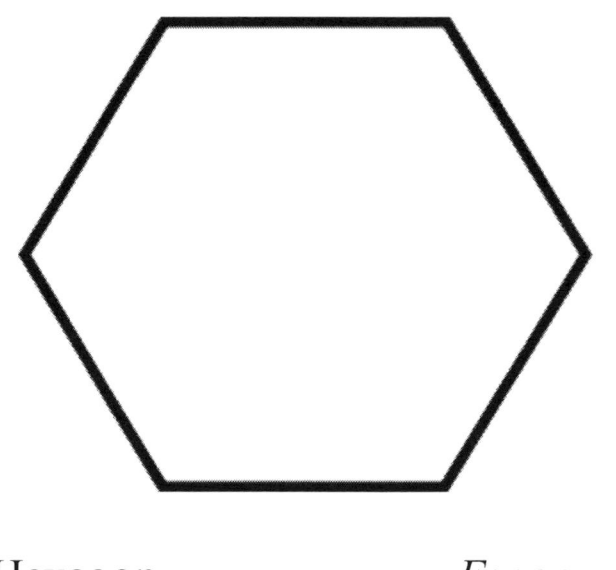

Hexagon - *Esagono*

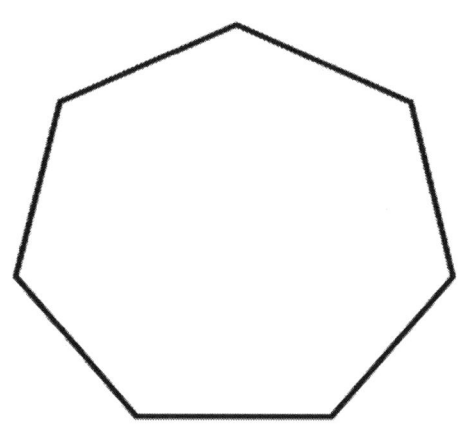

Heptagon - *Ettagono*

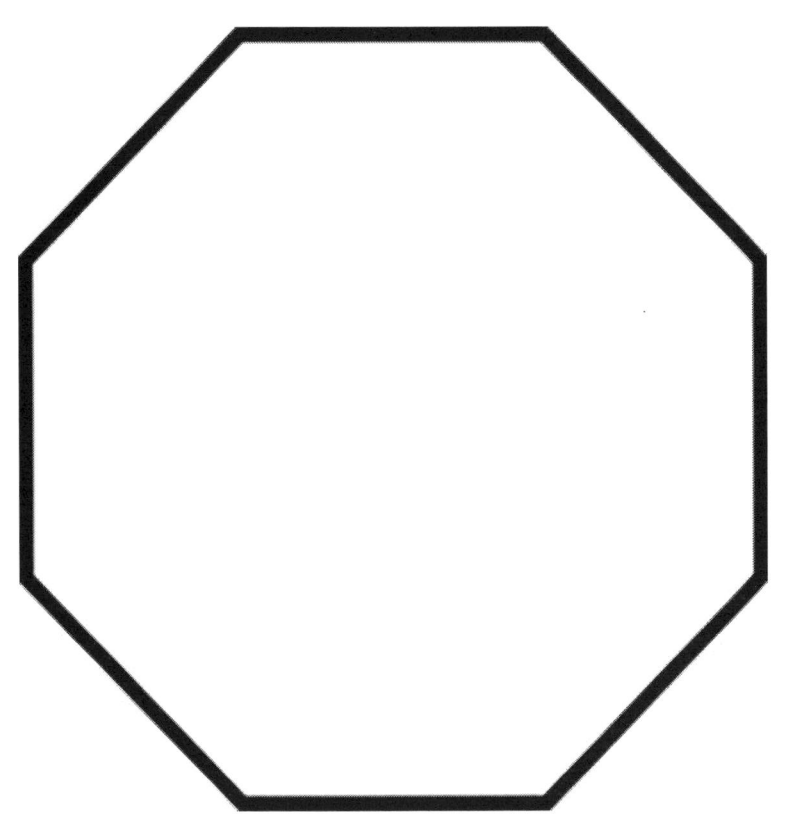

Octagon -   Ottagono

Fruits and vegetables / Frutta e verdura

Orange · *Arancia*

Apple · *Mela*

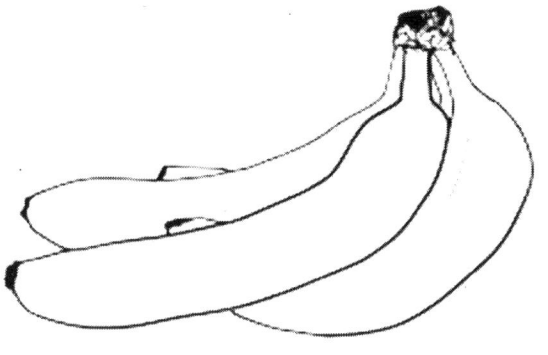

Bananas *Banane*

Carrot *Carota*

Cucumber *Cetriolo*

Pineapple *Ananas*

Lime · *Lime*

Lemon · *Limone*

Grapes　　　　　　　　　*Uva*

Pawpaw　　　　　　　　Pawpaw

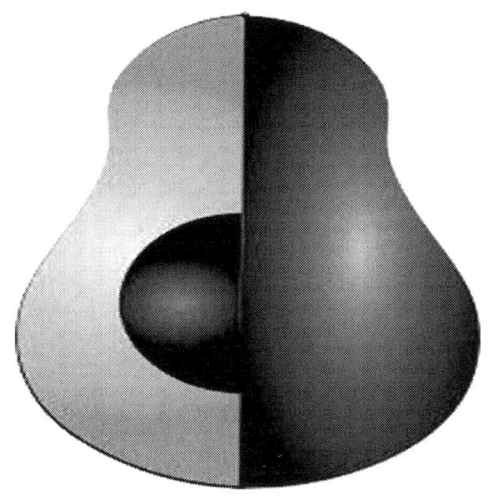

Pear   *Pera*

Mango   *Mango*

Body parts/ Parti del corpo

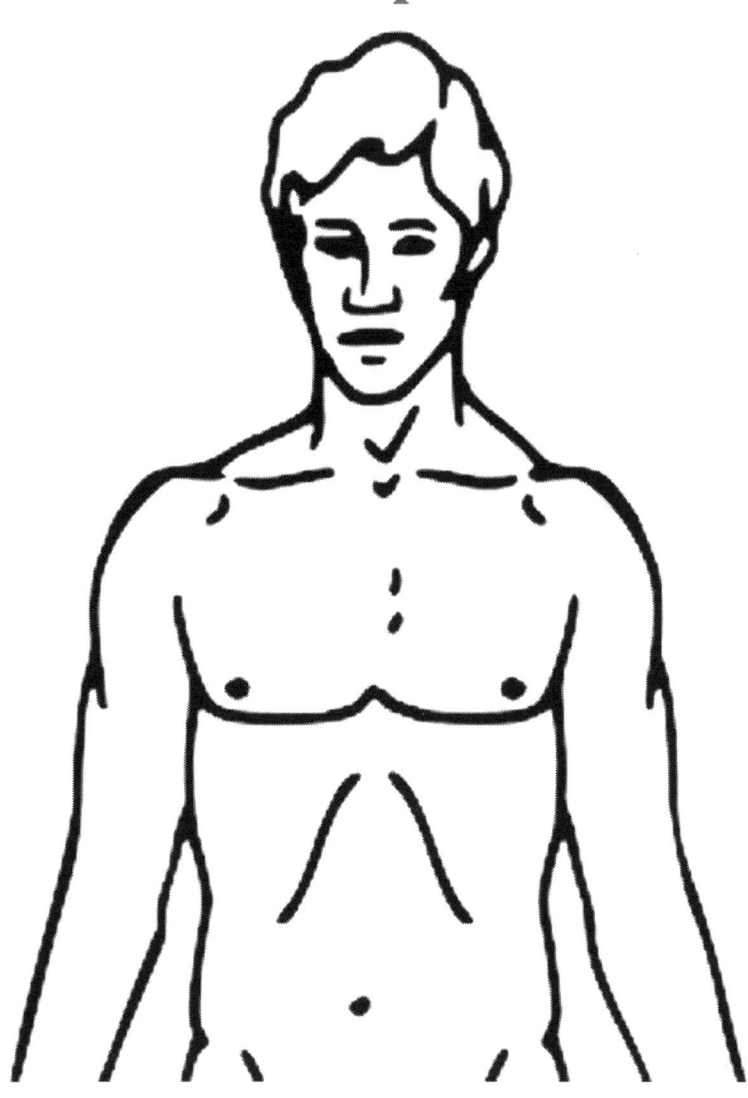

Eyes   *Occhi*

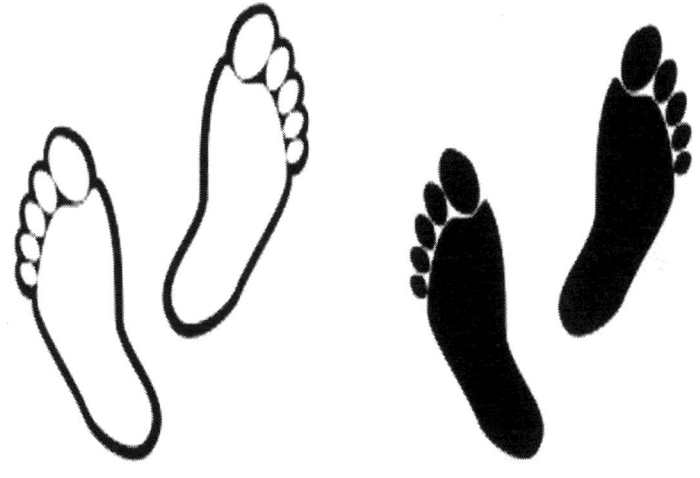

Toes   *Dita dei piedi*

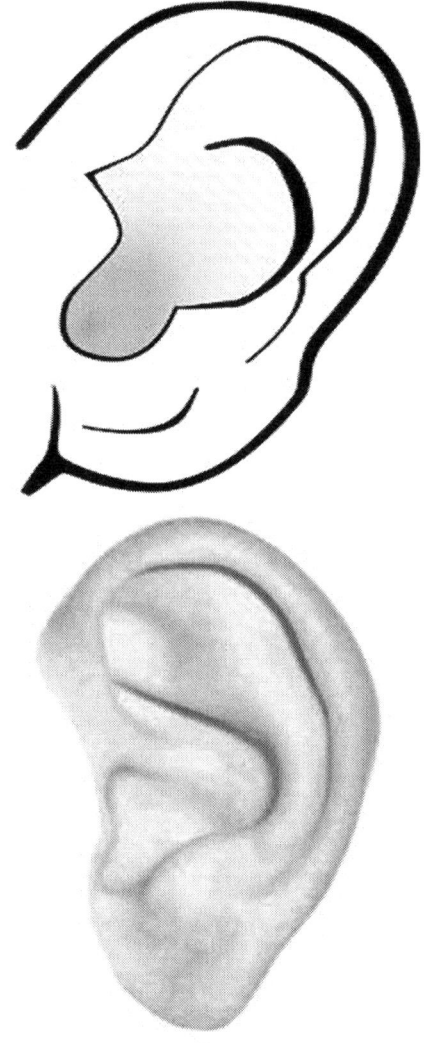

Ears   *Orecchie*

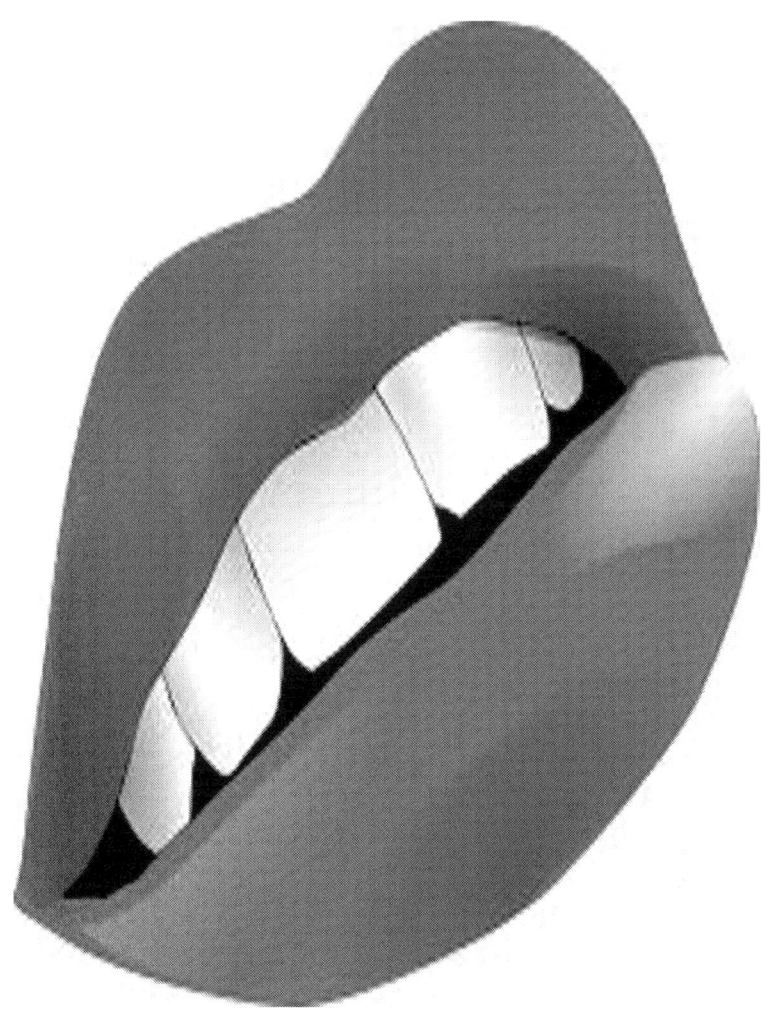

Teeth   *Denti*

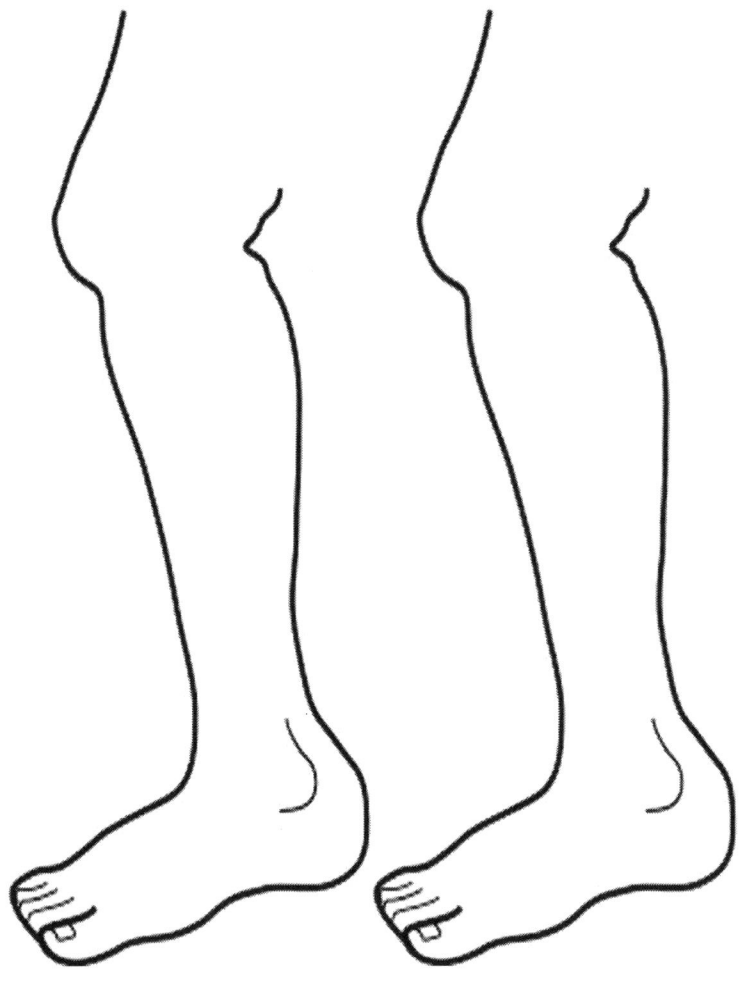

Legs   *Gambe*

Hands   *Mani*

Fingers   *Dita*

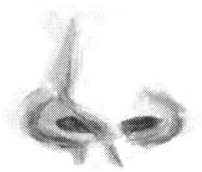

Nose   *Naso*

Knees   G*inocchia*

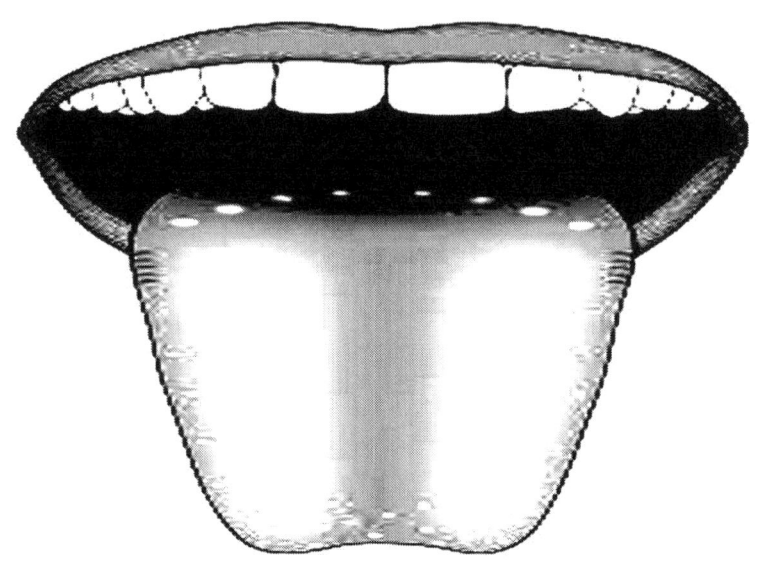

Tongue   *Lingua*

Days of the week/ **Giorni della settimana**

Noel : *Let's look at days of the week*
   Diamo un'occhiata ai giorni della settimana

Sunday   *Domenica*

Monday   *Lunedì*

Tuesday   *Martedì*

Wednesday   *Mercoledì*

Thursday   *Giovedì*

Friday   *Venerdì*

Saturday   *Sabato*

Days we go to school / **Giorni andiamo a scuola**

Noel: *Mondays we go to school* - Il lunedì andiamo a scuola

Tuesdays we go to school - Il martedì andiamo a scuola

Wednesdays we go to school - Il mercoledì andiamo a scuola

Thursdays we go to school - Il giovedì andiamo a scuola

Fridays we go to school - Venerdì andiamo a scuola

Saturdays we stay at home - Il sabato restiamo a casa

Sundays we go to church - La domenica andiamo in chiesa

Noel: *Mondays to Fridays, we go to school.* - Dal lunedì al venerdì, andiamo a scuola.

Noel: *Monday to Friday I go to school* - Dal lunedì al venerdì vado a scuola

Saturday I stay at home - Sabato rimango a casa

Sunday I go to church - Domenica vado in chiesa

Noel: *From Monday to Friday my teacher teaches me Mathematics and English*

Dal lunedì al venerdì il mio insegnante mi insegna matematica e inglese

The months of the year/ I mesi dell'anno

Noel: *Next is Months of the year*

Il prossimo è Mesi dell'anno

Noel: *There are twelve months in the year* - Ci sono dodici mesi all'anno

Twelve months of the year/
Dodici mesi dell'anno

January	*Gennaio*
February	*Febbraio*
March	*Marzo*
April	*Aprile*
May	*Potrebbe*
June	*Giugno*
July	*Luglio*
August	*Agosto*
September	*Settembre*
October	*Ottobre*
November	*Novembre*
December	*Dicembre*

Seasons of the year/ **Stagioni dell'anno**

Noel: *What about Seasons of the year?*

Che mi dici delle stagioni dell'anno?

Seasons of the year/ Stagioni dell'anno

Spring	*Primavera*
Summer	*Estate*
Autumn	*Autunno*
Winter	*Inverno*

- **Spring** Occurs In The Months of March, April and May.
- **Summer** starts from June to August.
- **Autumn** is from September, October and November and
- **Winter** is from December to February.

... La primavera si verifica nei mesi di marzo, aprile e maggio.

 L'estate inizia da giugno ad agosto.

 L'autunno è da settembre, ottobre e novembre e

L'inverno è da dicembre a febbraio.

Colors/ Colori

Red	*Rosso*
Yellow	*Giallo*
Blue	*Blu*
Brown	*Marrone*
Pink	*Rosa*
Orange	*Arancia*
Black	*Nero*
White	*Bianca*
Green	*Verde*
Cream	*Crema*
Gold	*Oro*
Silver	*Argento*

Animals/ Animali

Dog — *Cane*

Rat — *Ratto*

Lion — *Leone*

Tiger — *Tigre*

Hippopotamus — *Ippopotamo*

Monkey — *Scimmia*

Gorilla — *Gorilla*

Lizard — *Lucertola*

Cheetah — *Ghepardo*

Hyena — *Iena*

Other common words/ *Altre parole comuni*

Food — *Cibo*

Bedroom — *Camera da letto*

Kitchen — *Cucina*

Bathroom — *Bagno*

Backyard — *Cortile*

Park — *Parco*

School — *Scuola*

Beach — *Spiaggia*

Supermarket — *Supermercato*

Farm — *Azienda agricola*

Manufactured by Amazon.ca
Bolton, ON